For the Teacher

This reproducible study guide consists of lessons to use in conjunction with a specific novel. Written in chapter-by-chapter format, the guide contains a synopsis, pre-reading activities, vocabulary and comprehension exercises, as well as extension activities to be used as follow-up to the novel.

In a homogeneous classroom, whole class instruction with one title is appropriate. In a heterogeneous classroom, reading groups should be formed: each group works on a different novel on its reading level. Depending upon the length of time devoted to reading in the classroom, each novel, with its guide and accompanying lessons, may be completed in three to six weeks.

Begin using NOVEL-TIES for reading development by distributing the novel and a folder to each child. Distribute duplicated pages of the study guide for students to place in their folders. After examining the cover and glancing through the book, students can participate in several pre-reading activities. Vocabulary questions should be considered prior to reading a chapter; all other work should be done after the chapter has been read. Comprehension questions can be answered orally or in writing. The classroom teacher should determine the amount of work to be assigned, always keeping in mind that readers must be nurtured and that the ultimate goal is encouraging students' love of reading.

The benefits of using NOVEL-TIES are numerous. Students read good literature in the original, rather than in abridged or edited form. The good reading habits, formed by practice in focusing on interpretive comprehension and literary techniques, will be transferred to the books students read independently. Passive readers become active, avid readers.

Y0-COU-059

Novel-Ties® are printed on recycled paper.

The purchase of this study guide entitles an individual teacher to reproduce pages for use in a classroom. Reproduction for use in an entire school or school system or for commercial use is prohibited. Beyond the classroom use by an individual teacher, reproduction, transmittal or retrieval of this work is prohibited without written permission from the publisher.

Copyright © 1999 by LEARNING LINKS INC.

SYNOPSIS

In this sequel to *Shiloh*, Marty Preston settles into a loving friendship with Shiloh, a beagle he rescued from the abuse of Judd Travers. Marty's family has embraced Shiloh with their characteristic love and generosity, and he is flourishing after only a few weeks in his new home. Marty, however, will need more time to regain his father's trust after lying to protect Shiloh. He is also worried about his dog's safety now that hunting season nears. Judd Travers is drinking again and seems to bear a grudge against Marty and Shiloh.

Marty's parents, worried that Judd will hunt on their property while intoxicated, warn Judd to stay off their land. Since this engenders further ill will, Marty and his sisters are no longer allowed into the woods to play. Not only do the Prestons have concerns about Judd, but the entire community of Friendly and Tyler County are worried about his behavior.

One night Marty and his friend David Howard spy on Judd. When they see him drinking heavily and witness him shooting squirrels out of season, they make their presence known. Judd knows the identity of the boys, but luckily, in his drunken state, is unable to locate their hiding place.

Marty's father finds out he went to spy when Judd accuses him of scratching his truck and knocking over his mailbox. He is disappointed in Marty for making the situation more tense and is also unable to trust his denial completely. When Marty's little sister Becky is missing one evening after a game of hide-and-seek, Marty begins to question his decision to keep Judd's deer kill a secret. He is afraid that it has only allowed Judd to continue hunting and now perhaps hurt someone. To make matters worse, Judd's dogs get loose and kill a neighbor's cat and attack Marty's sister Dara Lynn. Judd accuses Ray Preston of releasing the dogs and demands Shiloh as a replacement. Marty's father refuses.

Marty has a short period free from anxiety that is interrupted when Judd takes a pot shot at him and Shiloh. Not wishing to upset his father, Marty keeps the incident a secret.

Judd's problems come to a head one night when Marty is wakened to a loud bang and the sound of Shiloh whimpering. Fearful for his dog's safety, he and his father go out to investigate. They find Shiloh near the site where Judd has crashed his truck. He is hurt badly, and if not for Shiloh, might have died. In spite of Judd's ugly nature, the community rallies around and tries to help him. Judd is neither readily accepting of these gestures, nor grateful.

Trying to teach him lessons in kindness, Marty continues to bring Judd gifts of food and gracious notes, and then finally pays a personal visit with a fearful Shiloh in tow. This gesture accomplishes its goal as Judd reaches out to Shiloh, not with a boot, but with a gentle touch.

PRE-READING ACTIVITIES

1. Preview the book by reading the title and the author's name and by looking at the cover illustration. This book is part of a trilogy. What is a trilogy? What do you think the title means? What do you think this book will be about?

2. With students in your class who have read *Shiloh*, the first book in the trilogy, fill in a chart, such as the one below, to record everything that is known about the main characters in the book. Add to this chart after you have finished the book.

Character	Description
Marty	
Marty's father	
Marty's mother	
Becky	
Dara Lynn	
Judd Travers	

3. If you have already read *Shiloh*, work with a partner to write a summary of the book. Then write an advertisement of "coming highlights" for the next book about Shiloh and Marty Preston. Predict what you think the future holds for Marty, Shiloh, and Judd Travers. After you finish the book, check to see if any of your predictions were correct.

4. With your classmates, discuss whether individuals have a responsibility to their community to reveal the activities of people who may be dangerous. Do they have this responsibility even if revealing the identity of dangerous people could put their own lives or the lives of their friends and family in jeopardy?

5. Have you ever lost someone's trust or stopped trusting someone else? Share what happened to cause this and how it made you feel. Was the trust ever regained?

6. Do you think it is acceptable to lie in certain situations? If so, describe such a situation. Suppose you were keeping a secret that protected someone who had done something wrong. How would you feel? What would you do if someone important to you, like your parents, asked you for the truth?

7. With your classmates discuss the nature of gossip. What effects does it have on people? Have you ever gossiped? How did it make you feel? What happens as gossip passes from person to person?

Pre-Reading Activities (cont.)

8. With a partner discuss why some dogs are mean and so many others are loving and gentle. What makes dogs behave so differently? Is it possible for a mean dog to become gentle? Why or why not? If so, how does it change?

9. Hunting is limited to certain times during the year. Why are these regulations in place? Why not allow hunting all the time or not at all? Is it as serious to hunt small game, such as squirrels or geese, out of season as it is larger game, such as deer or bears?

CHAPTER 1

Vocabulary: Draw a line from each word on the left to its definition on the right. Then use the numbered words to fill in the blanks in the sentences below.

1. weave
2. poachers
3. contented
4. spite
5. dwell
6. rile

a. hard feelings
b. people who hunt or fish illegally
c. irritate; anger
d. move back and forth, in and out
e. think about; focus on
f. happy; satisfied

. . . .

1. The hound began to _____ across the field, following the scent of the rabbit.

2. The sound of rattling papers will surely _____ the people sitting next to you in the theater.

3. My brother broke the video game out of _____ because he was disappointed not to get one of his own for his birthday.

4. I felt _____ once the job was complete and done to my best ability.

5. I offered the little girl a piece of candy so she would not _____ on her bruised knee.

6. If _____ are caught hunting on my land, they will receive fines.

Questions:

1. How did Marty repay Doc Murphy for repairing Shiloh's injuries?

2. How did Marty learn that Judd Travers was drinking heavily again?

3. Why did Ma think Judd was drinking?

4. What worried Ma and Dad most about Judd?

5. Why did Dad travel to Judd's house on Sunday evening?

Chapter 1 (cont.)

Questions for Discussion:

1. Do you think Marty and his family should be afraid of Judd?

2. What do you think happened at the meeting between Dad and Judd? Why didn't the author reveal exactly what happened?

3. Do you think Marty should tell his parents the secret about Judd and the doe?

Literary Devices:

I. *Dialect* — Dialect refers to local speech patterns that differ from standard speech. Find two examples of dialect at the beginning of the book.

_____

_____

_____

_____

Why do you think the author used dialect?

_____

_____

II. *Point of View* — Point of view in literature refers to the voice telling the story. It could be the author narrating or one of the characters telling the story. From whose point of view is this story told?

_____

How does this point of view make it difficult to reveal what occurs during Dad's visit with Judd?

_____

_____

_____

Writing Activity:

Write about a time when you or someone you know was in danger or felt threatened by another person. Describe the menace and tell how the issue was resolved.

CHAPTERS 2, 3

Vocabulary: Replace each underlined word or words with a more descriptive word from the Word Box that has a similar meaning. Write the word you choose on the line below the sentence.

WORD BOX		
barreling	beam	echo
gleam	restless	spare

1. After replacing the used batteries in his flashlight, Tommy put the <u>leftover, unused</u> batteries in the drawer.

   _____

2. The airplane followed the <u>ray of light</u> to guide it down for a landing.

   _____

3. The hunting dogs became more and more <u>uneasy</u> as they got closer to the fox.

   _____

4. The boys' voices seemed to <u>bounce off the walls</u> in the darkness of the cave.

   _____

5. The children came <u>running</u> out of the school to start their summer vacation.

   _____

6. My little brother had a <u>naughty look</u> in his eye as he snuck a cookie off the plate.

   _____

Questions:

1. Why did Marty tell Miss Talbot and his entire sixth-grade class about Shiloh?
2. Why did Marty worry about Shiloh while he was away at school during the day?
3. Why did Marty feel homesick the night he slept at David's house?

Questions for Discussion:

1. Do you think Marty's mother should have allowed Shiloh to roam free in the woods?
2. Should the police have curtailed Judd Travers' wild behavior and drinking?

Chapters 2, 3 (cont.)

Literary Device: Metaphor

A metaphor is a suggested or implied comparison between two unlike objects. For example:

> He [Shiloh] don't much care for the big yellow monster [school bus] that gobbles us up weekday mornings, and spits us out again each afternoon.

What is being compared?

_____

What does this suggest about Shiloh's feelings toward Marty?

_____

_____

Writing Activities:

1. Reread the short paragraph in Chapter Two where Marty described his dog greeting him after school. In the chart below, record the words and phrases that evoke each of the senses.

sight	
sound	
smell	
touch	
taste	

Now create a similar chart recording words and phrases to describe an event in your own life. Then use this chart as notes to write a paragraph in which the description makes the event come alive.

2. Write about a dream that seemed so real that you believed the events of the dream were really happening. Describe the dream in enough detail so that the reader can visualize it.

CHAPTERS 4, 5

Vocabulary: Draw a line from each word on the left to its definition on the right. Then use the numbered words to fill in the blanks in the sentences below.

1. incorporate
2. cowardly
3. slurred
4. ramble
5. grudge
6. ford
7. ruckus
8. transplant

a. speak aimlessly
b. feelings of anger or resentment
c. noisy commotion
d. combine legally
e. move something from one place to another (usually a bush or a plant)
f. shallow place in a stream
g. fainthearted
h. garbled; unclear

. . . .

1. If you do not give the speaker a five-minute limit, he will _____ on for an hour.

2. It would be better for the two smaller companies to _____ into a larger, more efficient organization.

3. Hoping that we can be friends one day, I try not to hold a(n) _____ when you hurt my feelings.

4. Sue's speech was _____ after she had an injection of Novocaine at the dentist's office.

5. Expecting a(n) _____ when the latest hit rock group arrived in town, the police were sent to the scene.

6. It is best to cross the stream at a(n) _____.

7. We will have to _____ the rose bush before the builders come to dig up the garden.

8. Afraid that my fellow soldiers would become aware of my _____ feelings, I hid my shaking hands in my pockets.

Chapters 4, 5 (cont.)

Questions:

1. Why did people sometimes leave cake or pie for Marty's father in their mailboxes?

2. What did Marty mean when he said that he felt his chest tighten?

3. Why did Marty have to be careful answering his mother's questions about his night at the Howards?

4. Why did Marty go with his father to deliver Judd's mail?

5. Why did Doc Murphy have Marty transplant some bushes for him?

6. What did Marty's reaction to the squirrel reveal about him?

7. Why did David and Marty feel sick inside?

Questions for Discussion:

1. Why was Marty so worried when he realized that hunting laws meant little to Judd Travers?

2. Do you think that kindness can fix anything wrong with humans or animals?

3. What did Marty mean when he worried that there "could be a Shiloh season and it could be any time at all"?

Writing Activities:

1. Imagine you are David Howard and write a thank you note to Mrs. Preston after the sleepover date. Describe the things you enjoyed while you were there.

2. Despite his fear of Judd, Marty speaks out when he sees Judd senselessly killing a squirrel. Write about a time when you witnessed something you knew was wrong. What did you do? Why? If you could, would you do anything differently?

Chapters 4, 5 (cont.)

Literary Element: Characterization

Characters in literature are revealed by what they say and do and by what others say about them. In the chart below, fill in information you have learned about Marty, his father, and Judd Travers. Continue to add new information as you read the book.

Character	What You Have Learned
Marty Preston	
Ray Preston	
Judd Travers	

CHAPTERS 6, 7

Vocabulary: Synonyms are words with similar meanings. Draw a line from each word in column A to its synonym in column B. Then use the words in column A to fill in the blanks in the sentences below.

A	B
1. misery	a. cheap
2. carcass	b. suffering
3. sly	c. play
4. meadow	d. field
5. miserly	e. shrewd
6. testy	f. corpse
7. romp	g. grouchy

. . . .

1. My brother becomes _____ whenever I borrow his baseball glove without asking permission.

2. We stood on a hill to observe the beautiful flowers growing in the expanse of _____ below.

3. The vultures made a meal of the _____ on the side of the road.

4. The teacher ended the students' _____ when she told them that they all had passed the test.

5. My sister is so _____ with her allowance, she has every penny she was ever given.

6. Detecting a _____ smile on your face, I could not trust your excuse for being late.

7. It was fun to watch the puppies _____ in the tall grass.

Questions:

1. Why didn't Marty think that he and David should reveal that they saw Judd kill a squirrel?

2. Why did Marty think he might have been responsible for Judd's return to drinking? Why did Marty's father disagree?

3. Why did Judd become angry when Marty told him that it was he and David on his property the night before?

Chapters 6, 7 (cont.)

4. Why did Marty decide not to tell his father about playing spy? How did Ray Preston learn about his son's "spying"?

5. Why was Marty dreading the talk about Judd's mailbox if he really didn't do it?

Literary Element: Conflict

The plot of a novel is the sequence of events that happen in the story. A conflict is a problem, often a struggle between opposing forces. A novel usually has one or more major conflicts that must be resolved before its end. In the chart below, list the conflicts that have occurred in the story so far. Add to the chart as you continue to read the book.

Conflict Type	Description	Resolution
Person *vs.* self		
Person *vs.* person		
Person *vs.* society		

Math Connection:

Marty complained that the math examples he faced in school had no practical value. Try to create word problems that describe a situation that you might face. Create one in which you would need to multiply a three-digit number by a two-digit number with a decimal point.

Create another problem in which you would need to divide a three-digit number by a two-digit number with a decimal point.

Writing Activities:

1. Mr. Preston believed he should have waited to talk to Judd when he was sober. Rewrite their conversation the way you think Marty's father hoped it would turn out.

2. Write about a time when you or someone you know lost the trust of another. Describe the situation that caused this to happen and tell whether faith in the individual was ever restored.

CHAPTERS 8, 9

Vocabulary: Analogies are equations in which the first pair of words has the same relationship as the second pair of words. For example: SWEET is to SOUR as SMOOTH is to ROUGH. Both pairs of words are opposites. Choose the best word from the Word Box to complete each of the analogies below.

```
                 WORD BOX

        listless        tremble
        lure            tug
        steep           wander
```

1. TRAP is to CATCH as TEMPT is to _____.

2. FAST is to SLOW as _____ is to ENERGETIC.

3. FLAT is to PLAIN as _____ is to CLIFF.

4. _____ is to RAMBLE as TWIRL is to SPIN.

5. _____ is to FEAR as WEEP is to SADNESS.

6. _____ is to PULL as SHOVE is to PUSH.

Questions:

1. Why did Marty count to three hundred to let the girls hide in their hide-and-seek game?

2. Why did Marty's legs almost give out when he remembered seeing Becky on the meadow path?

3. Why did Marty feel responsible for Becky's disappearance and possible danger?

4. Why did Marty's father wish he had handled the disagreement with Judd in a better way?

5. How did Shiloh become a hero on the night of Becky's disappearance?

Chapters 8, 9 (cont.)

Questions for Discussion:

1. Did Ma react fairly when she blamed Shiloh and Marty for Becky's disappearance?

2. Is it appropriate for boys to hug and kiss family members?

3. Why did Marty sleep well the night of Becky's disappearance?

Literary Device: Cliffhanger

A cliffhanger in literature is a device borrowed from serialized silent films in which an episode or chapter ends at a moment of heightened tension. In a book it is usually placed at the end of a chapter to encourage the reader to continue on in the book. What is the cliffhanger at the end of Chapter Eight?

_____

_____

Writing Activity:

Tell the story of the night of Becky's disappearance from the point of view of Marty's father or mother. Write about their worry and their subsequent relief.

CHAPTERS 10, 11

Vocabulary: Use the words in the Word Box and the clues below to fill in the crossword puzzle.

WORD BOX

accuse	loyal	protest
fierce	lunge	rabies
flinch	props	veterinarian
hepatitis		

Across

1. wild; violent in force
3. demonstrate disapproval
5. disease of the liver, characterized by jaundice
7. faithful to one's obligations
9. blame

Down

1. cringe; shrink back
2. someone who practices the medical and surgical treatment of animals
4. disease contracted from the bite of an infected animal
6. supports
8. make a sudden, forward thrust

Chapters 10, 11 (cont.)

Questions:

1. Why was it important that Shiloh be taken to the vet?
2. How did Doc Murphy help Shiloh relax in his office?
3. Why did Marty decide his report on veterinarians for the "Imagine the Future" project needed more work?
4. Why did Judd drive to the Prestons' farm? Why did he demand Shiloh be loaned to him?
5. How did Ma convince Judd to leave without Shiloh?

Questions for Discussion:

1. Do you think Shiloh would have come to Judd if he had continued to call him or perhaps whistle for him?
2. Do you think Marty's parents should have been tougher with Judd, or were they correct to remain polite?

Science Connection:

Do some research on any animal that you might like to have as a pet. Write a short informational article describing the care and feeding of this animal.

Writing Activity:

Imagine you are Marty's mother. Write a diary entry about the dog attack describing your fears and feelings during and after the attack.

CHAPTERS 12, 13

Vocabulary: Use the context to determine the meaning of the underlined word in each of the following sentences. Circle the letter of the answer you choose.

1. Although the police listened to <u>gossip</u> about the suspected burglars, they knew they needed facts and evidence.

    a. jokes   b. rumors   c. news   d. data

2. The <u>jolt</u> I received when someone slapped me on the back caused me to drop my books and fall down.

    a. light tap   b. heavy blow   c. sudden cry   d. anxious call

3. An <u>orderly</u> came to my room to make sure I was comfortable.

    a. sanitation worker b. messenger   c. hospital   d. assistant
                                              attendant

4. It is wise to <u>pause</u> and think carefully before making an important decision.

    a. wait briefly   b. stop short   c. forge ahead   d. sit down

5. You will notice that names are <u>posted</u> on all the doors so that you can identify the people in each of the offices.

    a. called   b. noticed   c. erased   d. listed

6. The teacher asked her two students to end their <u>quarrel</u> and share a book.

    a. friendship   b. battle   c. understanding   d. argument

7. A <u>quiver</u> of fear ran through my body as our car drove close to the edge of the cliff.

    a. fever   b. shudder   c. twitch   d. moment

Questions:

1. Why did Miss Talbot start a discussion about truth and gossip in Marty's class?
2. Why did Miss Talbot speak to Marty after school? How did Marty react to her suggestions?
3. Why did Marty worry about the way his father might settle his quarrel with Judd?
4. What decisions did Marty make on the day Judd took a shot at him?
5. Why did Marty tell Doc Murphy about "blackmailing" Judd in order to keep Shiloh?

Chapters 12, 13 (cont.)

Questions for Discussion:

1. What dangers might have ensued if gossip gave way to truth regarding Judd Travers and his dogs?

2. Should Marty's family have laughed over Grandma Preston's activities?

3. Should children keep important events secret from their families?

4. Did Doc Murphy give Marty good advice?

Literary Device: Cliffhanger

What is the cliffhanger at the end of Chapter Thirteen?

_____

What do you think has happened?

_____

_____

Writing Activities:

1. Write about a time when gossip overcame truth in your life.

2. Write about a time when a sight or sound you could not identify scared you. Describe the incident with enough detail so that the reader will experience your fright.

CHAPTERS 14, 15

Vocabulary: Read each group of words. Cross out the one that does not belong with the others. On the line below the words, tell how the remaining words are alike.

1. bravery   courage   timidity   fearlessness
   These words are alike because _____

2. unconscious   alert   unaware   senseless
   These words are alike because _____

3. gory   bloody   gruesome   exciting
   These words are alike because _____

4. ambles   marches   strolls   wanders
   These words are alike because _____

5. ruptured   burst   fractured   torn
   These words are alike because _____

6. solitary   lone   multiple   single
   These words are alike because _____

Questions:

1. What did Marty think had happened when he was awakened by Shiloh's yelping?
2. Why was Shiloh yelping in the middle of the night?
3. Why was Marty ashamed of his thoughts when he saw the accident?
4. Why did Judd owe Shiloh his life?
5. How did Marty's father react when Marty confessed to the "blackmail" and the shot Judd aimed toward him?
6. Why did Miss Talbot's idea of making a card for Judd meet with silence in her class?
7. According to Doc Murphy, why wasn't Judd kind to his dogs?

Chapters 14, 15 (cont.)

Questions for Discussion:

1. Why do you think Marty finally told his father about the way he "blackmailed" Judd and the time Judd shot at him?

2. Why do you think Judd's neighbors were kind to him after the accident?

3. Was Judd's behavior justified in light of his family history?

Science Connection:

Do some research on your own to learn about the geography of the world's oceans. Learn about the sites mentioned in the book: the Galapagos Fracture Zone, Continental Shelf, Bounty Trough, and Bonin Trench. Find a diagram of the floor of the Pacific Ocean and share it with your class.

Writing Activity:

Pretend to be a reporter on the scene of Judd's accident. Write a newspaper article that would accurately describe the accident based on facts and not gossip or speculation. Be sure to provide a short, attention grabbing headline that might appear on the front page of the newspaper.

CHAPTER 16

Vocabulary: Replace each underlined word or phrase with a more descriptive word from the Word Box that has a similar meaning. Write the word you choose on the line below the sentence.

```
                    WORD BOX

        burrowing          limp
        casserole          slunk
        eased              wretched
```

1. The hunter <u>carefully moved</u> closer to the deer so it wouldn't become startled and run away.

    _____

2. The fox <u>cowered and snuck away</u> through the bushes after being chased by the hound.

    _____

3. We watched the fox <u>digging</u> under the fence around the chicken coop.

    _____

4. After a fight for its life, we saw the <u>miserable</u> coyote leave the wolf behind.

    _____

5. The stalks of the tomato plant became <u>droopy and weak</u> in the hot summer sun.

    _____

6. I volunteered to bring a <u>mixture of food cooked in one dish</u> to the pot luck dinner.

    _____

Questions:

1. Why did Marty and his family start leaving food and notes for Judd?
2. Why did Marty think Judd ignored the gifts of food at first?
3. What did Marty really want to communicate in his letters to Judd?
4. How did Judd reveal that he had learned kindness?

Chapter 16 (cont.)

Questions for Discussion:

1. Why do you think Marty brought Shiloh to see Judd?
2. What do you think Judd found he needed in Shiloh?

Writing Activity:

Imagine you are Judd Travers and write a letter to Marty expressing how you feel about his family and what they have done for you since the accident. Tell how this has affected your feelings toward Shiloh.

CLOZE ACTIVITY

The following passage has been taken from Chapter Twelve. Read it through completely and then fill in each blank with a word that makes sense. Afterwards, you may compare your language with that of the author.

Pow!

Something hits the log so hard it _____,[1] and I don't know whether it's the _____[2] moving under me or the noise, but _____[3] tumble backward onto the ground. Shiloh hops _____[4] the log and scrunches down beside me. _____[5] know even before I can think it _____[6] somebody took a shot at us.

My _____[7] already pounding hard from the run, and _____[8] it's like to explode. Don't know whether _____[9] stay where we are or try to _____[10] up to Doc's house. Didn't see any _____[11] on at his place, so he's probably _____[12] even home. I'm afraid if I try to _____,[13] Shiloh will make himself a target for _____[14] out there.

And then I hear the _____[15] of an engine starting up. I know, _____[16] I lie there, leaves in my face, _____[17] it's Judd Travers's pickup turning around on _____[18] road and heading back over the bridge. _____[19] only when the truck is gone that _____[20] sit up. I crawl back over the _____[21] again, looking for the place the bullet _____,[22] and I find it—a small hole _____[23] round and clean as a gun barrel.

_____[24] let out my breath and pull Shiloh _____[25] my lap. I can feel my knees _____.[26] Judd must have been coming over the _____[27] when he saw me and Shiloh racing _____[28] the road. He probably pulled over, got _____,[29] and followed us with his rifle.

There are three main thoughts going through my head, all trying to get my attention at the same time: first, this is the closest Judd ever came to trying to hurt Shiloh or me; second, I don't know whether he was trying to kill one of us, but his aim was way off the mark, so maybe he was only trying to scare me—either that or he's drunk; and third, I'm not tellin' my dad.

POST-READING ACTIVITIES

1. Return to the predictions you wrote about this book in the Pre-Reading Activities on page two of this study guide. Were any of your predictions correct? What do you think the third book in the trilogy will be about?

2. Return to the character chart you began in the Pre-Reading Activities on page two of this study guide. Add any other new characters to the chart. Add additional information to the character names already on the chart. Compare your chart with those of your classmates.

3. Talk to personnel at a local Humane Society or the ASPCA regarding the services they provide. Ask about animals that are abused and the steps required to rehabilitate them so they are able to be safe and happy pets. Construct a bulletin board or informational packet. Organize a school fundraiser for local animal agencies or, if possible, volunteer to help at the shelter.

4. With partners, choose a favorite scene from the book and role-play. If necessary, have one person assume the role of narrator.

5. Judd Travers and Ray Preston have a disagreement that might have been prevented if it had been handled differently. Perhaps this has happened to you and a friend. Go back to the conversation referred to in Chapter One and described in more detail in Chapter Six. With a partner, discuss ways to better handle disagreements and role-play what Mr. Preston and Judd might have done to resolve their differences.

6. What does the title *Shiloh Season* mean? Think about what you have learned from the book and think of a new title. Draw a new cover for the book and write a brief summary that you would find on the back cover.

7. Marty decided to write to Judd in an effort to teach him kindness. Imagine you are Judd and write a letter back to Marty. The letter can be written before or after Marty brings Shiloh to visit.

8. In spite of Judd's personality, the Prestons and the community of Friendly rallied support for him when he was injured in the accident. How important is this spirit of helping? Does it exist in your community and school? Make a list of all existing community services and instances of social services individuals have offered to those in need.

Post-Reading Activities (cont.)

9. Make Zucchini Bread for your family and friends using the following recipe:

Zucchini Bread

What you need:

3 eggs

1 cup vegetable oil

2 cups sugar

1 tablespoon vanilla extract

2 cups shredded peeled zucchini (about 2 medium or 1 large zucchini)

3 cups flour

1 teaspoon salt

1 teaspoon baking soda

1 teaspoon ground cinnamon

1/4 teaspoon baking powder

What you do:

1. Preheat oven to 350 degrees.
2. Beat together eggs, oil, sugar, and vanilla.
3. Stir in shredded zucchini.
4. Combine remaining dry ingredients and add to zucchini mixture.
5. Mix well.
6. Pour into two greased 8" x 4" loaf pans and bake one hour.

    Chocolate variation: Replace 1/2 cup of flour with the same amount of baking cocoa.

SUGGESTIONS FOR FURTHER READING

Fiction

* Armstrong, William H. *Sounder*. HarperCollins.
* Byars, Betsy. *The Midnight Fox*. Penguin.
* Cleary, Beverly. *Dear Mr. Henshaw*. Avon.
* Cleaver, Vera, and Bill Cleaver. *Where the Lilies Bloom*. HarperCollins.
* Dahl, Roald. *Danny, the Champion of the World*. Penguin.
  George, Jean Craighead. *The Cry of the Crow*. HarperCollins.
* Gipson, Fred. *Old Yeller*. HarperCollins.
* Henry, Marguerite. *Misty of Chincoteague*. Simon & Schuster.
  Kjelgaard, Jim. *Big Red*. Bantam.
  Locker, Thomas. *Family Farm*. Dial.
* MacLachlan, Patricia. *Sarah, Plain and Tall*. HarperCollins.
  Morey, Walt. *Gentle Ben*. Penguin.
* North, Sterling. *Rascal*. Bantam.
* Rawlings, Marjorie Kinnan. *The Yearling*. Simon & Schuster.
* Selden, George. *The Cricket in Times Square*. Dell.
  Speare, Elizabeth. *Sign of the Beaver*. Dell.
* Steinbeck, John. *The Red Pony*. Penguin.
* Taylor, Theodore. *The Trouble With Tuck*. Avon.
* Wagner, Jane. *J.T.* Dell.
* White, E.B. *Charlotte's Web*. HarperCollins.
* _____. *The Trumpet of the Swan*. HarperCollins.

Some Other Books by Phyllis Reynolds Naylor

    The Agony of Alice.
    Beetles, Lightly Toasted.
    The Keeper.
    Reluctantly Alice.
    Saving Shiloh.
    Send No Blessings.
* *Shiloh.*
    A String of Chances.

* NOVEL-TIES Study Guides are available for these titles.

ANSWER KEY

Chapter 1

Vocabulary: 1. d 2. b 3. f 4. a 5. e 6. c; 1. weave 2. rile 3. spite 4. contented 5. dwell 6. poachers

Questions: 1. To repay Doc Murphy, Marty cashed in found aluminum cans and bottles, and he worked off the rest he owed during the summer. 2. When Judd in his truck nearly ran over Marty as he wove up the road, it was clear that he was intoxicated. 3. Ma thought Judd drank because he was unhappy with himself, particularly after his dog Shiloh kept running away to Marty. She also thought Judd resented the dog's preference for Marty as well as the boy's steadfastness in working despite his insults. 4. Ma and Dad worried that Judd, under the influence of alcohol, would be hunting and shooting recklessly in their woods. This might endanger their family and Shiloh. 5. Dad went to Judd's house to inform him that someone had been poaching on his land. He didn't directly accuse Judd, but indicated that the beer can left behind suggested that Judd was guilty.

Chapters 2, 3

Vocabulary: 1. spare 2. beam 3. restless 4. echo 5. barreling 6. gleam

Questions: 1. Marty told his class about Shiloh and Judd Travers on his first day of school in response to Miss Talbot's request that each student reveal something important. 2. Marty worried that an intoxicated Judd Travers might harm Shiloh, particularly since his mother didn't think it was fair to lock up the dog in the house. 3. Marty felt homesick because he missed his family a little, but missed Shiloh a lot.

Chapters 4, 5

Vocabulary: 1. d 2. g 3. h 4. a 5. b 6. f 7. c 8. e; 1. ramble 2. incorporate 3. grudge 4. slurred 5. ruckus 6. ford 7. transplant 8. cowardly

Questions: 1. People left cakes and pies for Marty's father in appreciation for his fine mail service and because they liked him. 2. When Marty's chest tightened, it revealed the fear he felt at the idea that Judd might try to take Shiloh back. 3. Marty had to be careful not to hurt his mother's feelings by talking about the fancier dinner and making it seem as if he preferred Mrs. Howard's cooking over her own. 4. Marty went along on his father's mail route hoping he would see Judd and have the opportunity to talk to him and make things right again. 5. Doc Murphy had Marty transplant bushes as part of his repayment plan for medical care of Shiloh. 6. Marty's reaction to Judd shooting the squirrel indicated that he cared for living things and was also courageous enough to try to speak out against their abuse. 7. David and Marty felt sick inside after witnessing the violent, senseless killing of an animal.

Chapters 6, 7

Vocabulary: 1. b 2. f 3. e 4. d 5. a 6. g 7. c; 1. testy 2. meadow 3. carcass 4. misery 5. miserly 6. sly 7. romp

Questions: 1. Marty didn't think that he and David should mention that Judd shot a squirrel because the authorities would not take action and it might further inflame Judd. 2. Marty thought he might be responsible for Judd's return to drinking because he imagined Judd missed having a boy around his house now that the work ended. Marty's father disagreed because he believed that Judd had deep-seated problems that had nothing to do with his son. 3. Judd became angry because he assumed Marty was not telling the truth. He assumed that it was Marty's father who had sent the boys and that they had maliciously scratched his truck. 4. Marty didn't tell his father about playing spy because he knew his dad would get angry with him for making a bad situation with Judd even worse. Ray Preston learned that his son had visited Judd's property when Judd called to accuse Marty of smashing his mailbox. 5. Marty didn't want to talk to his dad about the mailbox because he knew his father would have a hard time trusting him since he once lied about hiding Shiloh and now spying on Judd.

Chapters 8, 9

Vocabulary: 1. lure 2. listless 3. steep 4. wander 5. tremble 6. tug

Questions: 1. Marty counted all the way up to three hundred because Dara Lynn had hurt her leg and needed extra time to hide. 2. Marty's legs almost gave out when he remembered last seeing Becky on the path to the meadow because he was afraid she had gone there in spite of the warning the children had been given about hunters in general and Judd Travers in

particular. 3. Marty felt responsible if something happened to Becky because he did not turn in Judd for shooting the doe out of season, and now Judd was still hunting up in the meadow. 4. Marty's father wished he had handled the disagreement better because he was afraid that he had inflamed Judd's anger, causing him to hunt on the Prestons' property out of spite. 5. Shiloh was a hero because he discovered Becky and led Marty to the place where she had fallen asleep.

Chapters 10, 11

Vocabulary: Across — 1. fierce 3. protest 5. hepatitis 7. loyal 9. accuse; Down — 1. flinch 2. veterinarian 4. rabies 6. props 8. lunge

Questions: 1. Once the local newspaper reported there was a case of rabies in the county, Shiloh needed to be taken to the vet for shots. This was particularly important for dogs that had been confined as Shiloh had been under Judd's ownership because he might have been attacked by an infected animal and would have been unable to defend himself. 2. Doc Murphy spent enough time petting Shiloh and talking to him softly so that the dog stopped shaking and relaxed even as he got a rabies shot. 3. After hearing other classmates' reports and Miss Talbot's comments, Marty decided he should do more work on his own. 4. Judd demanded Shiloh because his second best hunter has been quarantined and he felt it was the Prestons' fault. 5. Ma convinced Judd to leave without Shiloh by agreeing not to press charges against the dogs that attacked and bit Dara Lynn.

Chapters 12, 13

Vocabulary: 1. b 2. b 3. c 4. a 5. d 6. d 7. b

Questions: 1. Miss Talbot discussed truth and gossip when the stories about Judd Travers' dogs were being blown out of proportion. 2. Miss Talbot talked to Marty about the need to make his country writing and speech conform to standard English. Marty was flattered by Miss Talbot's attention and sensitivity. He understood that he needed to work on his literacy skills in order to realize his goals in life. 3. Marty worried that his father, concerned primarily about the safety of his family, might agree to relinquish Shiloh. 4. Marty decided not to tell his father about the shot and became determined not to make himself a target again. 5. Marty talked to Doc Murphy about "blackmailing" Judd because he felt guilty that he had perhaps given Judd license to continue shooting out of season and putting himself and others in danger.

Chapters 14, 15

Vocabulary: 1. timidity — the other words refer to the ability to successfully face danger 2. alert — the other words all describe the state of not being aware of events going on around you 3. exciting — the other words describe gross, unsightly events 4. marches — the other words describe a slow way of walking 5. fractured — the other words describe a soft object or organ being damaged and opened 6. multiple — the other words refer to one object

Questions: 1. When he heard the yelping, Marty was afraid that Shiloh had been hurt by another animal or by Judd. 2. Shiloh was yelping to alert others that Judd's truck had smashed and rolled off the road and that Judd might be injured. 3. Marty was ashamed because he thought how much better things would be if Judd died or was injured badly enough not to hunt ever again. 4. Judd owed Shiloh his life because the dog did not give up until someone came to find him. 5. Marty's father did not say anything about the blackmail because the idea of his son being shot at was much more serious to him. 6. The idea of making a card was met with silence because none of the children liked Judd and did not want to be insincere when writing a card. 7. According to Doc Murphy, Judd was unkind to his dogs because he had never known kindness in his whole life and didn't know how to treat others with kindness.

Chapter 16

Vocabulary: 1. eased 2. slunk 3. burrowing 4. wretched 5. limp 6. casserole

Questions: 1. Believing that Judd had to be taught about kindness, Marty and his family, ignoring Judd's rebuffs, continued to leave him food and notes. 2. Marty thought Judd was like Shiloh who was once distrustful of kindness. He also believed that Judd felt unworthy and embarrassed by kindness. 3. Marty wanted to let Judd know that it was Shiloh to whom he owed his life in spite of the abuse the dog experienced at his hands. 4. Judd revealed that he had learned kindness when he opened his trailer door to Marty, his father, and Shiloh and then gently stroked the dog's head.